What do you like?

Written by Anna Owen

Collins

toast

an egg

cereal

What do you like for breakfast?

3

yoghurt

an apple

cake

What do you like for a snack?

5

a sandwich

pizza

baked potato

What do you like for lunch?

7

a banana

milk

biscuits

peanut butter sandwich

What do you like for tea?

pasta

curry

sausages

What do you like for dinner?

11

milk

water

hot chocolate

What do you like at bedtime?

13

What do you like?

Breakfast

 toast

 cereal

 an egg

Snack

 yoghurt

 an apple

 cake

Lunch

 a sandwich

 pizza

 baked potato

Tea

 a banana

 biscuit

 milk

 peanut butter sandwich

Dinner

 pasta

 curry

 sausage

Bedtime

 milk

 hot chocolate

 water

🐾 Ideas for guided reading 🐾

Learning objectives: Use one to one matching; Solve new words using meaning, syntax and print; track the text in the right order, pointing while reading; read on sight a range of familiar words; sustain attentive listening, responding to what they hear with relevant comments.

Curriculum links: Physical development: Keeping healthy and things that contribute to this

High frequency words: I, like, you, for

Interest words: breakfast, toast, snack, banana, lunch, milk, biscuit, dinner, pasta, bedtime, chocolate

Getting started

- Start a discussion with the children about their favourite foods. Write on the whiteboard *'I like ...'* and ask children to read and complete the phrase with their favourite food.
- Discuss different meals and what they are called, and write these on the whiteboard. What food do they eat at these meals?
- Walk through the book together, and discuss what is on each page – the different foods for each meal, the labels, the clock times and the child stating which of the food he/she prefers.

Reading and responding

- Ask the children to read the book independently and aloud up to p13.
- Observe, prompt and praise their use of one-to-one matching, reading high frequency words fluently and using the pictures and initial letters to help solve challenging words, e.g. *biscuit, chocolate.*
- Ask the children to look closely at the spread on pp14-15 and discuss what is eaten in each meal and at what time.

Returning to the book

- Ask the children in pairs to recap what the children in the book have for different meals. Discuss what they themselves would like and which meals in the book they would like. Would they choose different food?

how to
'harvest'
water

how to 'harvest' water

The art of saving water

National Trust

First published in the United Kingdom in 2011 by
National Trust Books
10 Southcombe Street
London
W14 0RA

An imprint of Anova Books Company Ltd

Packaged by Susanna Geoghegan

ISBN: 978 1 907892 00 4

A CIP catalogue record for this book is available from the British Library.

19 18 17 16 15 14 13 12
10 9 8 7 6 5 4 3 2 1

Printed in China by Kwong Fat

This book can be ordered direct from the publisher at the website
www.anovabooks.com, or try your local bookshop. Also available
at National Trust shops and www.nationaltrustbooks.co.uk.

Contents

Recycling water

Water and air, the two essential fluids on which all life depends, have become global garbage cans.

Jacques Cousteau

Water is fast becoming one of our most precious commodities. As consumption increases worldwide with growing demand and the effects of climate change, our freshwater resources are being depleted.

Water is not actually disappearing: the amount of water remains fairly constant within its water cycle, but our water-rich lifestyle is making an unprecedented demand on freshwater resources. This in turn is damaging the natural cycle of the water system and unbalancing the geographical distribution.

> **Growing population + climate change + water-rich lifestyle = yearly increase of water consumption**

The global water shortage relates to the discrepancy between where rain falls and where people live. In densely inhabited areas, renewable water resources are being over-stretched, which leads to localised water shortages and the need to use rivers, which would otherwise not support these communities, as further water sources. In fact, estimates suggest that by 2025 around 2 billion people will be living in water-short regions if water consumption continues at the same rate.

What can I do?

By changing your daily water habits on a domestic and workplace basis and encouraging others to do the same, you can make a difference to future generations who will otherwise struggle hard to survive.

Water saving helps to contribute to the international efforts to reduce water consumption and is not only low-maintenance but cost-effective.

By simply adapting your lifestyle and more importantly, your way of thinking about water, you can lower your water and electricity bills, help reduce greenhouse gas emissions, limit the damage to wildlife in rivers and wetlands and, vitally, help preserve natural freshwater levels. And it can all start by just turning off the tap while you brush your teeth …

The players

The global water crisis has become a top priority amongst governmental and non-governmental institutions. They are attempting to combat water pollution and inform the public about the necessity of saving water. However, increasing awareness of water issues amongst politicians and professionals cannot bring about an overall change in attitudes towards water wastage; we all need to take care of our natural resources.

For details of some of the organisations and charities working on water issues, see 'Resource pool' on page 74.

Where does our water come from?

'All the water that will ever be is, right now.'

National Geographic, October 1993

Let's talk about the water cycle …

Water is constantly moving. Evaporated from the land and oceans by the sun's rays, water as a liquid becomes water vapour, a gas. When it reaches the atmosphere, this vapour condenses into droplets of water which form clouds and eventually fall as rain.

This rainwater is freshwater, which flows through rivers and streams back towards the ocean, irrigating the land and providing drinking water along the way, until it is evaporated once again from the sea. It is a cycle, which naturally replenishes itself.

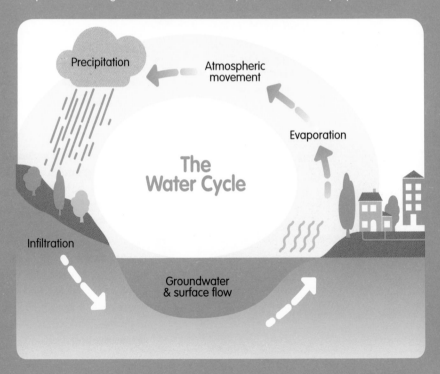

But if the water cycle is constant, why do we have a water crisis?

It's true that the volume of water on earth never changes: there is approximately 1,386 million cubic kilometres of water. However, only a minuscule 2.5% of this is freshwater, most of which is inaccessible as it is trapped in glaciers, ice, snow and permafrost.

> These are challenging times for the water sector particularly with the uncertainty caused by climate change. The most vulnerable parts of the country are the areas most reliant on groundwater.
>
> Denis Peach, UK Groundwater Forum Chair, 2010

So what about our day-to-day water?

Accessible freshwater comes from four main sources:

1. **Groundwater is found beneath the earth's surface in rock fractures and soil pore space. Most UK drinking water comes from groundwater.**

2. **Surface water is water collected from the ground and from rivers, lakes and wetlands.**

3. **Rainwater is water collected from the external surfaces of buildings or hard-standing areas by diverting the flow to a storage tank.**

4. **Recycled water/reclaimed water is wastewater that has been treated to remove solids and some impurities, or domestic wastewater from our kitchen and bathroom, and can be used for landscape irrigation.**

Whereas groundwater and surface water need to be professionally accessed, rainwater and recycled water can be used at your own discretion. The quantity of rainwater you collect and then reuse can make a significant dent in your annual water bill, should you follow a few water harvesting tips.

Are you letting your water and your money flow down the plughole? >>

How much water do you use?

Have you ever stopped to think how much water you use every week?

Try calculating how much water you use on average per week. The table opposite provides a few averages for the water consumption of daily household activities.

Yet it's shocking to think that these figures don't represent the average household the world over.

The industrialised world with its swimming pools and carwashes and garden sprinklers consumes far more water on a daily basis than less developed nations.

Although consumption depends on obvious differences such as climate and agricultural needs, the most worrying element is wealth.

In poor areas where water needs to be carried from wells or must be purchased, the household requirements for water are much lower.

Daily household activities:
typical water usage

Activity	Average weekly use	Litres used
Bath	2	80 per bath
Flushing the toilet	35	8 per flush
Gravity shower	7	35 per shower
Power shower	7	80 per shower
Brushing your teeth with the tap running	14	Minimum 6 litres per brush
Washing machine	3	65 per wash
Dishwasher	4	25
Watering the garden	1	540
Washing car with bucket	1 (4 buckets)	8 per bucket = 32 litres
Washing car with hosepipe	1	400–480

Your water footprint

Your water footprint is made up of two components – direct water and indirect water usage.

Your direct water footprint refers to the freshwater consumption and pollution that you control directly – what you use, as shown in the table.

Your indirect water footprint, sometimes called virtual water, silent water or embedded water, refers to the water consumption and pollution from the production of goods and services you consume.

See www.waterfootprint.org for further information on how to calculate your water footprint.

Water pollution
Rivers, streams and seas have always formed a natural drainage system which absorbs and cleanses waste matter...

However, the quantity of waste material being flushed into our water system, much of which is non-organic or toxic, is polluting water resources which are unable to break down such materials.Within the developing world, around 90% of all sewage is pumped – untreated – directly into water sources, endangering not only human life through disease, but damaging wildlife, which can no longer survive in stagnating waters. However, industrial waste such as fertilisers, pesticides and toxic by-products pose an even greater threat to our water systems.

Your own household contributes to the pollution of the world's water supply
When you flush toiletries, washing powders, chemicals and food waste down the drain, even more water is required to dilute these pollutants and

make wastewater drinkable. Yet by simply using environmentally friendly cleaning and bathing products, or limiting the quantities of chemicals you allow to go down the drain, you can help control the excessive pollution that is affecting the global water cycle. In addition, your skin will thank you for using environmentally friendly products. Harsh and perfumed detergents can play havoc with sensitive skin.

Fact: The number of dead zones (areas in which marine life cannot survive) in the world's oceans increased by 30% between 1995 and 2007.

What can I do?

Never throw litter, paint, oil, or other substances not intended to be in the water system, down the sink or toilet.

Use environmentally friendly versions of washing powder, cleaning products and toiletries. Choose phosphate-free detergents, as phosphates cause harmful algae blooms in rivers and lakes.

Do not over-use pesticides and fertilisers that can run off into water sources. Wildflowers and grassed areas along streams can help prevent chemicals running off into the water.

Never throw litter into rivers, lakes or oceans. If you see litter around these locations, pick it up and bin it.

Harvesting water inside

This government's aim for housing and planning is eco equality. We have introduced new standards for the way we plan, design and build homes for the future, like bringing water efficiency into Building Regulations for the first time.

Rt Hon John Healey MP, Minister for Housing and Planning
(Waterwise Water Efficiency Conference, 2010)

We all understand the importance of saving and harvesting water, but what can we do on a day-to-day basis to reverse this growing problem?

18

Our daily lives at home and at work are constantly dictated by our water usage, so with only a few simple changes in attitude and action, you can become water-wise and support global change.

From the kitchen to the bathroom, from laundry to leaks, to the items in your shopping basket, to the houses that we build, this section will give you some handy hints on how to successfully save water and ultimately reduce your water bills.

Although water harvesting is an essential component of developing a greener lifestyle, you may also want to consider other elements of your domestic lifestyle which could be adapted to help the environment. Saving electricity in particular, from using energy-saving lightbulbs to switching to greener electricity providers, helps to save water as it reduces your indirect water footprint.

Start by installing a water meter. Being able to monitor your usage is an excellent way of becoming more water conscious. If you are a water-saver and harvester, then having a water meter installed may be a cheaper option than continuing with national water rates. Your local water authority should provide you with a meter free of charge.

Simple changes made by many = big difference

19

Saving water in the kitchen

Whether you're boiling potatoes, washing the dishes or making a pot of coffee, food preparation in your kitchen requires an unprecedented quantity of water.

With the kitchen tap and dishwasher alone requiring up to 14% of your household water intake, it's easy to waste water just by leaving the tap running whilst rinsing your vegetables. Although we are all now particularly conscious of germs and the importance of washing fruits and vegetables, there are some techniques you can employ to both preserve water and maintain a healthy kitchen lifestyle.

Be boil-smart

Reuse the water from boiling vegetables and pasta. Instead of throwing the used water down the sink, use it to rinse plates to save on washing-up water.

If using a dishwasher, rinsing also means that you can use an economy cycle. Boiled water can also be used to kill off those pesky weeds growing through the cracks in your paving or patio, or leave it to cool to water the houseplants.

Turn your hot water bottle green

If it's chilly, fill your hot water bottle with the water from boiling vegetables. It'll be nice and warm and won't require you to boil more water in the kettle!

21

Reuse that mug

Don't keep reaching for clean crockery – cut down on washing-up by reusing your mug for that second cuppa.

Get your jugs out

Leave a jug of water in the fridge rather than leaving the tap running every time you need cold water. Waiting for cold water can waste up to 10 litres of water a day! (Waterwise UK)

Proportion

Don't overfill saucepans with water. Only boil what you need and make sure that you use the smallest possible saucepan size for your food.

Defrost, don't douse

Try not to thaw frozen foods under running water. Instead defrost them in a microwave, or better still, take them out of the freezer the night before.

Hand washing?

If you're hand washing dishes, never leave the tap running, but instead fill a bowl with warm soapy water. Rinse off in a separate bowl and if the rinse water isn't too soapy, dispense with it on the garden. Alternatively, if you use a dishwasher, always ensure that it is full of dirty dishes before you turn it on, in order to maximise the amount of clean dishes per water cycle.

Use a sink strainer

Don't use your sink as a waste disposal unit. Any food that you blithely toss in the sink needs to be removed at the treatment plant further downstream and can block drains and sewers, leading to possible flooding. Bin your scraps and compost any fruit and vegetable peelings.

Just a squirt

Don't be heavy-handed with washing-up detergent: try using half the amount you normally do. It will be sufficient and it will cut down on the rinse water.

Change your cooking technique

Try stir-frying vegetables, or roast them when you have a joint in the oven. Steaming vegetables can use less water than boiling them: better for the environment and as they'll retain more nutrients, better for you!

Myth: Dishwashers use more water than hand washing. Wrong! This is a common misconception: depending on the dishwasher, these machines can actually save you water! Make sure, however, when you buy a new dishwasher, that you check the energy rating to ensure that it's water efficient.

Tea time

Everyone loves a good cuppa – according to the UK Tea Council, people in the UK drink around 165 million cups of tea a day – but there are a few easy ways to make your brew more efficient.

Make sure that you only boil as much water as is needed. Fill the kettle initially by measuring out how many cups you require. After a while you'll recognise the weight appropriate to the number of cups. By doing this you'll not only be saving on water, but you'll dramatically reduce the energy required to boil the kettle each time!

If you're in the market for a new kettle, try buying an eco kettle which promises lower energy use and allows you to set the temperature of the water and how many cups you boil.

We drink around

165 million
cups a day

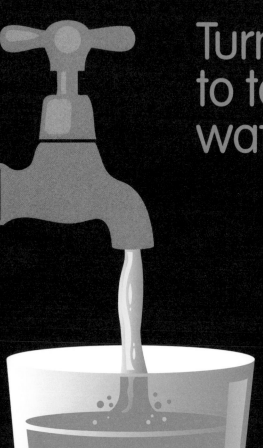

Turn on
to tap
water

Have you ever stopped to think about how much water and energy are needed to create a plastic bottle of water?

Between 3 and 7 litres of water are used to make and fill an average litre bottle: precious resources which are being squandered, considering that UK tap water is of one of the highest qualities in the world.

If plastic bottles were reused and recycled then this wouldn't be such a pressing issue – however with the majority of bottles ending up as litter, the time has come to return to drinking tap water and encouraging others to do the same.

Tap water at the National Trust
A growing number of Trust cafes, tearooms and restaurants are joining a campaign to promote tap water. The Trust has always had tap water available, but we are now making it more easily seen through a range of posters in selected cafes and branded flasks and bottles.

There are a number of reasons we are promoting tap water more than ever before:

It's safe and tasty and free: **The tap water in the UK is safe and healthy to drink, in fact among the best quality in the world. In blind taste tests many people could not tell the difference between bottled water and tap water.**

Water is a precious resource: **A one-litre plastic bottle may actually require 3–7 litres of water in the process of making and filling the bottle.**

Caring for the environment: **The plastic waste can often end up as litter, which can get washed into rivers. Did you know that in the Pacific Ocean there's a carpet of floating plastic the size of Europe? Transporting bottled water creates 33,200 tonnes of CO_2 in the UK alone, equivalent to the annual energy consumption of 6,000 homes.**

Leading the way: **Other organisations and businesses are realising that promoting tapwater is good for the environment and good for their reputations.**

Examples include Liverpool City Council, which has banned bottled water in the workplace since January 2007, and the London On Tap campaign, which involves many London restaurants. It is supported by the Mayor of London, Boris Johnson, who has said: 'I am pleased to offer my wholehearted support to this campaign to encourage Londoners to choose tap water when they are eating out.'

In addition, free tap water will be provided throughout the London 2012 Olympic venues.

The safety regulations for tap water are often far more rigorous than for bottled water. The frequent testing required by the water authorities means that there is no need to worry about the quality of your tap water.

When you're eating out you can save money and the environment at the same time by asking for a jug of tap water for the table. Restaurants must provide the option of tap water and you can report those who do not to the Consumer Council for Water.

By switching to tap water the average bottled water drinker could save themselves hundreds of pounds a year!

If you are concerned about the quality of your area's tap water, invest in a water filter. That way you can feel secure that your drinking water is clean and tastes good and help the environment at the same time. You can use the simple jug method which uses a filter cartridge through which the water is passed, or the plumbed-in undersink system which gives you filtered water directly from the tap.

Fact: It is estimated that globally more than 1.2 billion people do not have safe drinking water, 2.4 billion lack sanitation facilities, and 1,000 children die every day as a consequence of waterborne diseases.

The safety regulations for tap water are often far more rigorous than for bottled water ...

Buy them loose

Nowadays everything we buy comes packed, wrapped, vacuum-sealed and with a bow to finish. It looks all shiny and fresh and tasty, seducing you to buy, but have you ever stopped to consider how much water goes into your food before it even enters the kitchen?

Average quantity of water needed to produce the following everyday items:

One A4 sheet of paper	10 litres of water
One slice of bread	40 litres of water
One glass of beer (250ml)	75 litres of water
One cup of coffee	140 litres of water
One glass of milk	200 litres of water
One kg of sugar	1,500 litres of water
One cotton shirt	2,700 litres of water
One kg of beef	15,500 litres of water

Your water footprint begins long before you turn on a tap, with the water needed to produce the products you buy and create the packaging it comes in. Some manufacturers are beginning to display their water footprint, but it's not a legal requirement yet, so you may have to do your homework to find out how much water has been used to produce your favourite items. By simply avoiding overly packaged products, saying no to free plastic bags and understanding the implications your indirect water footprint has on the environment, you can help change the over-exploitation of water.

As nature intended

Fruit and vegetables have their own natural packaging. Pop them directly into a basket or reusable bag and say NO to that extra plastic and/or moulded polystyrene casing.

31

Buy in bulk

Buying larger quantities of dried foods like flour and cereals reduces the amount of packing you buy, especially as many items can be bought loose and stored in your own reusable containers.

Taste the difference

If you are a juice drinker, make a rough calculation of how many containers of fruit juice you buy annually. Probably quite a few. By switching to making your own, you will not only be helping to reduce the number of plastic bottles and cartons that need to be manufactured and disposed of, but you will also be reducing the amount of water that is used to reconstitute juices that are made from concentrate. In addition, juicing is a great way to use up any fruit that has been sitting in the fruit bowl for too long and has lost its pick-upable, 'Come and eat me' allure. Throw it all together and discover a new world of flavours.

Love a takeaway?

Try eating in instead. The throwaway takeaway lifestyle consumes an unparalleled quantity of packaging. Be classy and use a plate.

Recycled logo

If packaging is unavoidable, look for the recycled logo. At least these products are made from recycled materials and can in turn be recycled.

Footprint maths

Do some water footprint maths. Try substituting large water footprint goods for products with a small one. You could swap meat for vegetables, or try drinking tea instead of coffee.

Buy local

This great catch phrase is not to be confused with 'shop local'. To buy locally means to buy produce that has been farmed or produced locally, whereas the shop local campaign promotes shopping locally regardless of the origin of the product.

We must recognise how the UK's water footprint is impacting on global water scarcity.

We should ask whether it is right to import green beans – or even roses – from a water-stressed region like Kenya, for example. The burgeoning demand from developed countries is putting severe pressure on areas that are already short of water. Our virtual water footprint is critical and we need to give it far more attention.

Professor Peter Guthrie
University of Cambridge

Although buying locally may not be any more energy– or water–efficient, it does mean that we are not depleting supplies in those exporting countries that may be water-poor.

Grow your own

Things that can be grown in your kitchen or on window sills include herbs such as parsley and basil. You can even try sprouting your own seeds such as cress, mung beans and fenugreek – they make an excellent accompaniment to salads. Packed with vitamins, minerals and amino acids, most sprouts can be harvested within 1–3 days. Visit an organic food store and investigate the huge variety of sprouting seeds that are available.

Saving water in the bathroom

Nothing beats the simple pleasures of a warm shower or a relaxing bath, but your bathroom habits may be responsible for up to 20% of your household water usage.

You don't need to compromise your cleanliness to reduce your water bills.

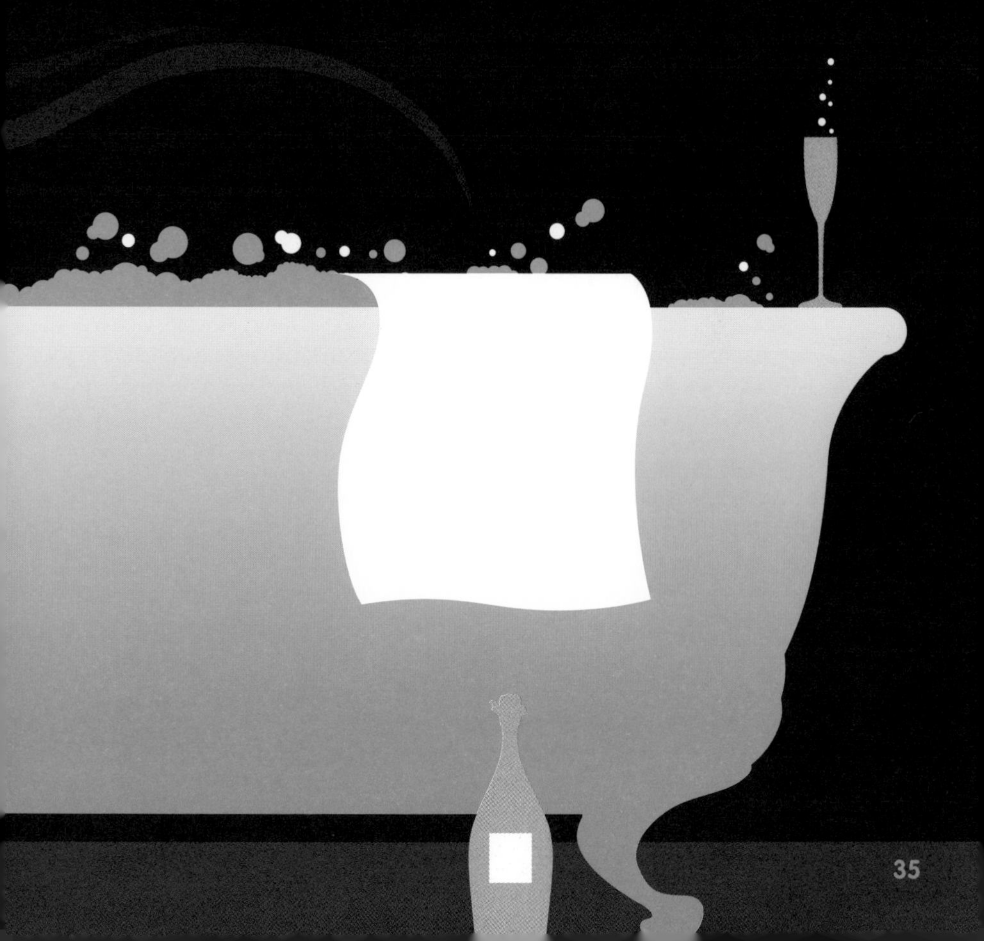

How to 'harvest' water

Bath vs. shower

Does it take less water to take a shower or have a bath? If your shower is above your bath, conduct a simple experiment: next time you have a shower put the plug in the tub and see how much you use. The Environment Agency, however, recommends short showers, not baths. Their research indicates that a five-minute shower uses about a third of the water of a bath. But power showers can use more water than a bath in less than five minutes.

Bathtime buddies

Let children share baths: not only does it make bathtime more fun, but it saves water. With an average bath requiring approximately 125 litres of water, it makes sense to share.

Showering alone?

Try taking a bucket into the shower with you: look out for the fold-away-flat plastic buckets designed expressly for water collection. Sounds odd, but the water that normally goes down the drain can provide a substantial drink for your plant pots outside. This is especially useful if your shower takes a while to heat up, as the cold water which is so unappealing to us is a godsend to your thirsty flowers. The same theory goes for using the sink whilst washing dishes or shaving. Just try not to use too many chemical products.

Close shave

Try rinsing your razor in the sink, not under a running tap. It'll do the same job but use far less water.

With an average bath requiring approximately 125 litres of water, it makes sense to share

Take fewer showers

We're not suggesting you walk around with a fragrant odour, but do think carefully about whether you really need more than one shower a day.

Invest in a low-flow showerhead or flow regulator

A low-flow showerhead reduces the amount of water per shower significantly, without compromising the water pressure of your regular showerhead. Lower water usage also means less energy required to heat up the water. A flow regulator is a small gadget suitable for non-electric mixer showers or bath mixer taps and is fitted between the shower hose and the mixer. So simple to do, there's no need to call a plumber.

Time yourself

Set a timer when you take a shower and leave it out of reach. You'll be gently reminded to turn off the water or face enduring the never-ending chiming.

A little dab will do you

Notice how your hairdressers only ever use a small dab of shampoo? It's not because they're stingy, but because your hair only needs a pea-sized amount. A great foamy lather doesn't make your hair cleaner, it just requires vastly more water to rinse it off. Saving yourself this lather not only prevents further pollution of the mains water, but will also save you money on shampoo.

Ready? Set? Go!

We all know the person who spends hours in the shower, uses all the hot water and gets on everyone's nerves.

So how long should you run water in the bathroom for?

Shower: Five minutes, or the time it takes to wash your hair, sing a couple of songs and go … In fact your skin will be grateful to you for spending less time under hot water. Hot water and soap causes skin to dry out and you'll be reaching out for the moisturiser.

Sink: Never leave the tap running. It uses approximately 6 litres of water in the time it takes to brush your teeth!

TIME-O-MATIC

39

Potty training

Toilet humour might be funny, but you should never joke about toilet water wastage.

It might be a delicate subject, discussing the to-ings and fro-ings inside your bathroom's walls, but the average toilet uses around 8 litres of water with every flush, a quantity which accumulates up to around a quarter of all clean water used daily in the home. There are, however, a few tricks that can reduce the amount used for flushing:

Keep a 'hippo' in your bathroom
If your toilet is a pre-2001 model, try fitting a 'hippo' or other displacement device.

You could try filling a small bottle with water and placing it inside the toilet tank. This will lessen the quantity of water used each time you flush.

Alternatively, you can use displacement bags available from DIY stores. Contact your local water authority or water company to see whether they supply any water efficiency products for free.

Think about the throne
If you're purchasing a new toilet, ensure that it has a low-flush rating or a dual-flush system that reduces the water usage to between 4 and 6 litres. You could even look into the possibility of installing a composting toilet.

Remember, remember!
Never flush anything down the toilet that isn't either digested, or toilet paper! Cotton wool, face wipes, tampons, sanitary pads and cigarette butts are for the bin.

Ask yourself …
if you need to flush every time.

Try it
Chaps, when you're using a public bathroom, use the urinal rather than the toilet as it uses far less water.

Displacement device for toilets
(Pre-2001 cisterns)

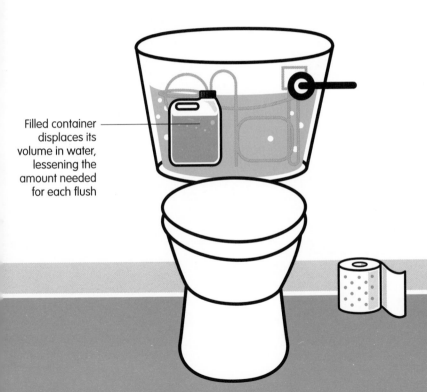

Filled container displaces its volume in water, lessening the amount needed for each flush

Laundry day

We're all glad that we no longer need to hand wash clothes and put them through the mangle, but despite technological advances the average washing machine still uses around 50 litres of water with every wash.

Unfortunately there is a huge degree of variation in water usage depending on your machine, so think carefully about your water bill before you buy a new one! Laundry now accounts for around 15% of domestic water use so follow these guidelines to reduce your laundry water consumption.

A full load please!
Always wash a full load of laundry. The capacity of your washing machine is often larger than the average load of washing, so make sure you maximise your machine's potential. If you only have a small load, use the half load function on your machine.

Efficiency rating

When buying a new washing machine, always check the efficiency ratings so you get the most efficient machine you can afford.

Read the manual!

Some washing machine cycles are more environmentally friendly than others, so do your homework.

Separated vs. non-separated

Not all coloured clothes need to be separated. In fact, after an item of clothing has been washed a few times there is very little chance the dye will run. By not sorting your clothes into separate colour washes, you will save yourself both water and money.

Turn it down!

Use a low temperature wash which requires less energy to heat the water. Modern detergents are designed to wash efficiently at 30°C.

Magnetism

Magnetic laundry balls work by ionising the water inside your washing machine, which is said to wash clothes more efficiently as soap powder is no longer required and water is saved because clothes don't need to be rinsed after the initial wash.

Good to know:

According to Waterwise UK the best washing machines should have a water efficiency of less than 7.5 litres per kilogram.

The waterless washing machine

Believe it or not scientists have developed a prototype of a washing machine that uses 90% less water than a conventional machine. Instead of water, plastic beads are used to suck up the dirt and stains, taking a hefty chunk out of your household water bill.

Self-cleaning clothes

Scientists have been experimenting with coating clothes fibres in titanium dioxide nanocrystals which break down dirt and stains when exposed to sunlight. Imagine the water and time you'd save never having to wash clothes again!

Leaky suspects

It's the look of sheer despair when you return home to a rather large, soapy puddle flooding your living room floor.

The whodunnit moment. A leaky trail points in the direction of a suspiciously gurgling, clunking washing machine …

However, there are a few DIY basics you can teach yourself to prevent and counter those leaks, saving water and possibly preventing further catastrophes...

Leaky culprit case No. 1

How can I tell if my toilet's leaking?

Food colouring. We're not suggesting you bake your troubles away, but adding a few drops to the toilet cistern could help you solve the problem. Add the colour and don't flush the toilet for at least one hour. If the colour shows up in the toilet bowl after an hour, you'll know you've got a leak.

If you're not a handyman, ring a plumber who knows which washers and seals are right for different toilets, or if you are good at DIY, take the specific parts to your local DIY shop or plumbing store. Remember to repeat the colour test afterwards to ensure that the leak is fixed!

Who you gonna call?

Although water by-laws make householders responsible for the good maintenance of their water systems, some water leakages are the responsibility of the water companies.

Report the following to your local water company or council:

- Flooding from roads and public drains
- Flooding from burst water mains outside your house
- Flooding from a main river

Inside a typical domestic tap

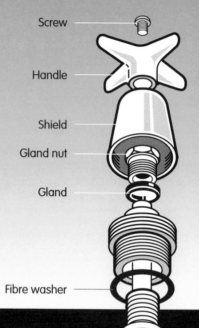

Screw

Handle

Shield

Gland nut

Gland

Fibre washer

Washer plate

Tap washer
This is probably the culprit if you have a leaky tap!

Tap body

Leaky culprit case No. 2

'Drip, drip, drip goes the tap...'

There's a reason that dripping water is used as a form of torture. You may think that you need a professional to fix that dripping tap but it is in fact a pretty easy piece of washer-changing DIY, and the sooner you fix it, the easier it is …

Here's how:

1 Turn off the water supply. Usually the supply knob is under the sink or connected to a pipe between the sink and toilet.

2 Place a crescent-shaped spanner on the head of the tap, loosen and remove it.

3 Look at the inside of this removed piece or where the piece was attached, to find the washer (it looks like a flat rubber doughnut). Remove the washer.

4 Clean the inside of the tap and the connections of all grime and limescale; vinegar does this well.

5 Take the old washer to a DIY shop and buy a replacement of the same size and shape. Attach the new washer to the tap head, making sure that it is flat against the head and not buckled.

6 Hand screw the head back onto the tap, making sure that the washer doesn't get caught inside the grooves. Tighten again with the crescent spanner.

7 Turn the water supply back on and run the tap for 30 seconds. Turn the tap off and see if it still drips!

What is
greywater?

Greywater is the water run-off from the shower, bath and washing machine and can, if managed carefully, provide an additional source of water for the garden during times of drought.

• •

However, whether you use this method is dependent on the cleaning products you use. A build-up of chemicals from detergents, or fats from soap, in your soil can be detrimental to your plants, so check the labels of the products you use.

Harmful chemicals found in laundry detergents are chlorine and phosphorous, and salt which is used as a bulking agent and totally unnecessary in the process of cleaning your clothes.

Switch to more eco-friendly products and accustom yourself to using less.

Kitchen water generally is too polluted with food particles and micro-organisms to be used on the garden, but the water in which you rinse your fruit and vegetables is safe to use.

Greywater tips:

- Never use greywater contaminated by faecal matter.
- Never let children play with greywater and always wash your hands after handling it.
- Do not store greywater for long periods, especially in warm weather when bacteria and algae grow more quickly.
- Do not water the same area of the garden every time. Rotate between several areas.
- Do not use greywater to water vegetables that you intend to eat raw.
- Stop using greywater if it appears to be damaging your plants.
- Only use greywater in non-potable water outlets.

> Water efficiency is unique in that it has an important role to play in tackling climate change as well as adapting to it – 5% of the UK's total greenhouse gas emissions come from heating water in homes for cooking, bathing and cleaning, and almost 1% of total UK emissions is accounted for by the water industry's own processes, including pumping and treating of water and wastewater. So wasting less hot and cold water will reduce emissions.
>
> **Maria Adebowale,**
> Chair of Waterwise (Waterwise Water Efficiency Conference, 2010)

'Green' building standards

Day-to-day rainwater harvesting techniques are now developing out of good personal habits into a fashionable, architectural and engineered element of modern house building. New building standards are calling for the incorporation of rain-harvesting technologies in new builds, which add value in the eyes of the new owners and provide an essential component in making a house environmentally friendly. Using rainwater to flush toilets and irrigate gardens is becoming an increasingly common feature in eco-conscious designs, especially in areas subject to drought conditions.

By installing harvesting systems, buildings can adhere to the government's new eco ratings, and sustainable homes which achieve a 'zero-carbon' standard will be granted a stamp duty exemption by the chancellor. Visit www.direct.gov.uk for further information. Although the new code is not obligatory in building practice as yet, the financial implication for house owners using a rain harvesting system is dramatic enough to have swayed public opinion to the

Typical rain collection system

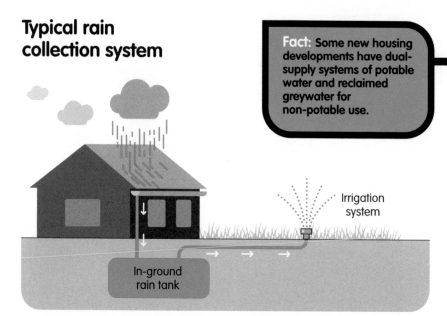

Fact: Some new housing developments have dual-supply systems of potable water and reclaimed greywater for non-potable use.

Irrigation system

In-ground rain tank

extent that 9 out of 10 house owners believe that rain harvesting is a good idea and would be more likely to buy a house with rain-harvesting potential.

Interested in adapting your home? Go to www.communities.gov.uk for more

details about how to adhere to the new green building regulations in the UK or try the UK Green Building Council, www.ukgbc.org, to see what is happening about making our overall built environment greener.

51

Water conservation in the garden

We all know that gardens can flourish with regular watering, but this means that plants become highly dependent on these artificial feeds, especially during the summer months.

There are a few basic rules that should be adhered to when planning a new garden or maintaining the one that came with the house you live in. A successful garden should be viewed as a long-term project and it would be wise to consider water-saving techniques at the outset. Think about how you use your garden.

Do you enjoy the indoor–outdoor lifestyle, in which case a large decking or patio area with several potted plants may serve you better than extensive flowerbeds? Are there children whose games will wreak havoc on the lawn, in which case a tougher, drought-resistant lawn should be favoured over the classical high-maintenance varieties? Do you have a large garden, in which case you could assign a section as a wild meadow area and plant up with bee-loving flowers and grasses? This area will not need watering and will help our fast-diminishing bees and other natural pollinators.

What is xeriscaping?

Xeriscaping is the practice of landscaping using drought-tolerant plants. The term derives from the Greek word Xeros, meaning 'dry'.

Even if you do not live in a particularly dry environment, it makes sense not to use plants that require more water than the plants that naturally flourish in your area. Planting in sympathy with your environment makes for a healthier environment; besides, stressed plants are more prone to pests and diseases which often require treatment with chemicals, which in turn get absorbed into the atmosphere and our soil.

Fact: Drought-resistant does not mean no water!

Plant according to conditions
Take a look at the annual rainfall and temperature charts for your area. If you live in an area of low or sporadic rainfall do not invest in thirsty plants.

Check the soil composition and plant according to what will do well naturally in your particular area. Trying to establish a bog garden in an exposed dry site is doomed to failure and is a waste of time, money and effort. Working with nature will be far more rewarding than fighting against it. Remember, nature has several of your lifetimes to reject inappropriate planting decisions. Garden with integrity and you will be saving a significant amount of water.

Plants for a low-water garden

When buying plants consult the staff at your local garden centre as they will be knowledgeable about what is most suitable for your area. A general rule of thumb for low rainfall areas is to look for hairy, waxy and very small leaves as they reduce water loss through evaporation, and fat leaves which store water for use in the dry times. Opposite is a list of common plants that can tolerate sustained dry conditions.

Plants for

Abelia

Achillea (Yarrow, of which there are many varieties and colours)

Agastache (Hyssop)

Agrostemma githago (Corn cockle)

Allium

Anenome (Windflower)

Asters

Aubretia

Aucuba (Laurel)

Berberis (of which there are many varieties and colours)

Bergenia (of which there are many varieties and colours)

Buddleja (Butterfly bush)

dry conditions

Campanula (Bell flower)

Ceanothus

Centaurea cyanus (Cornflower)

Choisya (Mexican orange blossom)

Cistus

Cordyline australis (Cabbage tree)

Cornus (Dogwood)

Cosmos

Cotoneaster

Crocosmia (Montbretia)

Cytisus (Broom)

Dianthus (of which there are many varieties and colours)

Echinacea (Coneflower)

Echinops (Globe thistle)

Eryngium (Sea holly)

Erysimum (Wall flower)

Escallonia

Euphorbia (Spurge, of which there are many varieties)

Geranium (of which there are many varieties and colours)

Helianthemum (Rock rose)

Hypericum (St John's Wort)

Iris (of which there are many varieties and colours)

Lavandula (Lavender, of which there are many varieties)

Myosotis (Forget-me-not)

Nigella (Love-in-a-mist)

Origanum (Oregano and Marjoram)

Papaver (Field poppy)

Pelargonium (of which there are many varieties and colours)

Perovskia (Russian sage)

Physalis (Chinese lantern)

Potentilla

Rosmarinus officinalis

Salvia (of which there are many varieties and colours)

Scabiosa (Pincushion flower)

Sedum (of which there are many varieties and colours)

Solidago (Golden rod)

Syringa (Lilac)

Thymus (Thyme)

Verbascum

Vinca (Periwinkle)

Yucca filamentosa

There are plenty of books on water saving in gardens, including *Thoughtful Gardening: Practical Gardening in Harmony with Nature* (also published by the National Trust) and some excellent online resources to help you.

Maximising water in the garden

Here are some tips for helping your garden:

Water butts

Collect as much rainwater as possible by installing water butts. Not just one, but several. Wherever there is a sloping roof and downpipe, a butt can be fitted and when there is a hosepipe ban you will be very grateful to have several strategically placed water butts around

The Golden Equation
One millimetre of rain to one square metre of roof = **one litre of rainwater.**

the house and shed: they will make watering by hand a lot less tiring.

Trellises and climbers provide an easy way to conceal water butts if you are worried about their appearance. They are easy to fit and by connecting two together, the overflow from the first will fill the second. You will be surprised how quickly they fill even during a brief shower. In addition, fit a rain diverter, a small device that directs excess water to the drains when your butts are full.

You can try contacting your local water authority for a free water butt, or even build one yourself, but make sure that you use the largest tank you can accommodate to maximise your water-harvesting potential.

Connect your butts

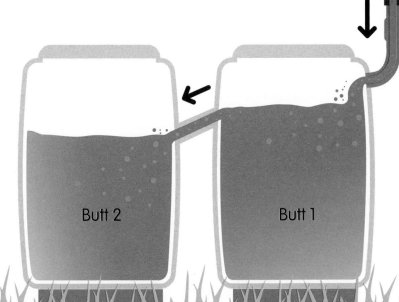

Butt 2

Butt 1

Water butt tips:

Some water companies provide free or reduced price water butts; do your homework and you could literally save a barrel-load.

Link your butts together to divert overflowing water. Always keep butts covered to reduce water loss through evaporation and to prevent leaves and bugs getting in.

Want to build your own water butt? You'll need a plastic, metal or wood container, a drill and some hosepipe valves. Search online for more detailed instructions.

Evening watering

Water in the evening when evaporation will be at its lowest, giving plants longer to absorb the water. It's also when the garden is at its most fragrant. And check the weather forecast – if rain is predicted, hold off on watering. Do not water on windy days as a high percentage of your effort will evaporate.

When to water

Examine the soil at a depth of 30cm at various and different situations around your garden. If the soil feels damp then it is unlikely that watering is necessary. If you are in an area of clay, it is difficult to establish if watering is needed, as clay feels damp even when dry.

Effective watering

Don't randomly splash water over the beds; water to the root of the plant and allow the water to be absorbed by the soil, otherwise you will waste water as run-off. Watering the leaves achieves little, as most will disappear through evaporation.

Soak, don't sprinkle

A good soak is far better than frequent sprinkles of water. Frequent light watering causes plants to shallow root, rather than putting down deep water-seeking roots. This does not stand them in good stead for periods of dry weather.

A stress-free start

Make sure that before planting a new addition to your garden, you give it a good soaking, preferably overnight. Watering young plants well so that they have a stress-free start in life will ensure that as adult plants they will have a better survival rate in more adverse conditions.

Watering systems

There are several very effective and timesaving watering systems that you can use for your flowerbeds, pots and lawn that require no more than a trip to your garden centre and no particular DIY skills to put together. One is the 'leaky' pipe system, which can be positioned just under the soil or on the surface. The principle is based on laying down a continuous length of hose through the area of the garden that requires watering. It can be attached to the mains or to a water butt. Made of porous rubber from recycled car tyres,

the water, as the name suggests, 'leaks' through the permeable material and with the use of various connectors, it allows you to water exactly where you need it. This is a very discreet method of watering, as it is easy to camouflage the hose around shrubs or with a covering of bark chippings.

If you go away for any length of time, you can fit an automated timer to water at designated times of the day. This is particularly important for pot plants that can dry out more quickly, although adding water-retaining gel crystals to the soil can reduce this.

Leaky pipe system

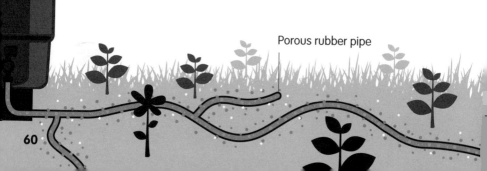

Porous rubber pipe

Drip line

The root system of a tree extends far beyond its trunk and in order to effectively water, follow the outer edge of the canopy.

Buckets galore

On days of heavy rainfall put out as many buckets as you can. Your plants will do better on rainwater than tap water and there are many that suffer

Tree drip line

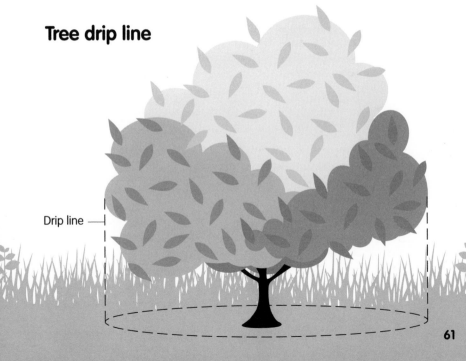

Drip line

from the regular application of treated water, especially houseplants which positively dislike the resultant lime build-up in the soil around them.

Love your broom
Forget about hosing paths and driveways; sweep them – it's much better for the planet and your fitness levels.

Groupies
Group plants with the same watering needs together to avoid overwatering some, while underwatering others. Being water-wise means that you will become more observant of the individual needs of the plants in your house and garden.

Plant in spring
Don't plant during the summer months. Newly planted areas or newly laid lawns won't survive without frequent watering if you plant them in summer. Set out plants and lawns as early in spring as possible, so that they develop good roots early, and if a dry period sets in, these should have top priority for whatever water is available.

Don't support weeds
Keep your garden free of weeds. Weeds on the whole are more resilient than your cultivated plants and their presence will reduce the amount of water uptake available for your plants.

Keep it light
Regularly hoe, to keep the soil loose and able to absorb water. Water will run off hard, compacted earth.

Mulch
Mulch your garden with a layer of bark chippings, well-rotted leaf mould or organic matter. Make sure that the leaf mould is well rotted, or else you will find that the leaves provide a barrier to the soil's uptake of water.

Goodness of compost

Add organic matter to the soil. A bucketful per square metre of compost, leaf mould and manure will help the soil retain its moisture. If you don't make your own, then it's a good time to start. Making your own compost will noticeably reduce the amount of rubbish you put out for collection, as well as keep your garden maintenance costs down. Composting is not a difficult or smelly art if you remember just a few basic rules such as using only uncooked fruit and vegetable scraps; only small quantities of grass clippings (too much and your compost will become smelly and slimy); and of course, your garden waste. Mixing 'green' and 'brown', such as shredded newspaper, will help keep a good balance.

There are plenty of books on the subject, including *How to 'Cook' Compost* (also published by the National Trust) and some excellent online resources to help you.

Low-water lawns

Choose varieties that are better suited to dry conditions, like fescue grass or smooth-stalked meadow grass. Consider having a 'mixed' lawn, that includes clover to grow with the grass and which will remain green longer during dry spells as well as encouraging pollinating insects. Instead of turf, you might consider an aromatic carpet of creeping thyme or lawn chamomile.

Let the grass grow longer in dry spells to help keep moisture in the soil.

Use a longer cut setting when mowing the lawn and try to cut it less often to reduce its need for water. It will also recover from dry spells more quickly.

As with plants, soak rather than sprinkle: a more thorough soaking will establish a deeper root system that can better withstand dry periods.

Aerate your lawn at least once a year so water can reach the roots rather than run off the surface.

Ponds

Ponds are a wonderful way of encouraging wildlife into your garden and providing birds with a reliable source of water. Just remember to create an easy access route for them to take water. There are just a few things to remember to make your pond green and water-friendly.

Make sure that you have installed a re-circulating pump so that you do not have to rely on rainfall or worse still, top-ups from the water mains. In addition, fish do not thrive in chlorinated water.

If you need to top up with tap water, add only small amounts so that your fish are not overwhelmed by a sudden change in their environment.

Use trickling or cascading fountains as they lose a lot less water to evaporation than those spraying water into the air.

When cleaning out ponds or fish tanks, give the nutrient-rich water to your plants.

Deeper water, shady areas and surface plants will reduce water loss through evaporation.

There are plenty of books on the subject, including *Ponds* (also published by the National Trust) and some excellent online resources to help you.

Thinking outside the box

Handy hints that you might not have thought about ...

Order tap water at a restaurant rather than bottled water. Restaurants (including those at National Trust properties) are responding to the shift in consumer awareness.

Staying in a hotel? Try reusing your towels rather than letting them be washed after one use. Many hotels have adopted a green policy by leaving a note in your room asking you to indicate whether you require a fresh towel but for those that have not, it's up to you to set an example.

Empty your pet's water bowl onto plants, not into the sink.

Romantic weekend away? Save water and get intimate by sharing a shower.

Just finished a slushy, icy coffee drink? Throw the ice into the garden, not into the sink.

Trainers a little dirty? Why not wipe them clean instead of putting them through the washing machine.

Freshwater is good to drink for about a week. There's no need to throw out that glass of water by your bed every morning, but if you do, pour it into a pet's bowl, or into a pot plant.

Educate your children and support their ideas about saving water. They learn a lot about water saving at school and are often more water-wise than adults. They are the future of our planet and the sooner they develop healthy, environmentally friendly habits, the sooner action will take place to save our natural resources.

Encourage your friends, family and business to try out some water-saving techniques. Low-maintenance tips such as a displacement device in a toilet are easy and cost nothing but an empty plastic bottle!

The future of water harvesting

There is no single silver bullet for water security. Water management must be looked at in a holistic way, from 'cloud to coast' including all forms of water – in the soil as well as in rivers and reservoirs. Reducing demand will be important but so will developing engineering solutions to create new, sustainable sources of water and promote efficiency in current practices.

Professor Peter Guthrie, University of Cambridge

Recycling water doesn't stop at home. The future of harvesting water lies in the efforts made on a global level to recycle water for both domestic and agricultural use. As around 1.2 billion people worldwide are still without safe drinking water and the average cost of water extraction is continually increasing, the conservation of water resources is a pressing issue the world over.

Particularly drought-ridden areas, such as Australia, have started to use reclaimed water for the irrigation of pastures, tree plantations and general agricultural uses, which would otherwise not be sustained by natural resources.

The United Nations' Millennium Development Goals are pushing for improvements in water and sanitation across the globe. However as these goals encourage greater food production and require increased sources of irrigation, new water-saving and water-accessing technologies must be used to achieve these ambitions.

This chapter will look briefly at some of the methods currently being explored to address this global phenomenon.

If there are methods to help improve the world water crisis, why isn't more being done?

Unfortunately, despite the best efforts of authorities, scientists, engineers and global organisations, there are still many issues which have to be tackled before constructive action can take place.

What issues are facing water authorities worldwide?

Corruption

Corruption adds 30% to the price of connecting to a water network in developing countries as a breathtaking 20–40% of water-sector finances are being siphoned off by dishonest practices. On a household basis, this corruption has a knock-on effect on aspects such as education, as children are forced to leave school to help their families collect water.

Privatisation of water

The privatisation of the water service has become a highly contentious issue, as many believe that water is a human right which should not be a source of private profit. Although the World Bank and IMF suggest that privatisation is advantageous due to the technical efficiency of the private sector and frequent mismanagement of the water service by governments, the challenge of providing an affordable service to low-income consumers becomes of paramount importance under a privatised scheme.

Shared resources

With 13 river basins shared by five or more countries, the potential for conflict over these precious water resources in times of drought or agricultural expansion has always been of extreme concern. The Nile, which flows through ten different countries, is now subject to the Nile Basin Initiative which hopes to maintain cooperation between those countries and prevent conflict over the exploitation of shared water resources.

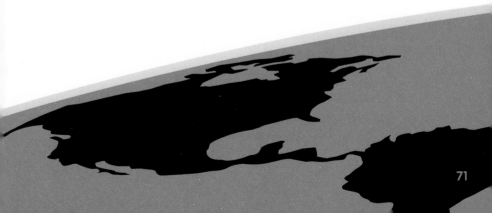

Aquifer recharging

What is an aquifer?

Aquifers are layers of water-holding permeable rock found underground, from which freshwater or groundwater can be extracted using a well. They are a crucial resource in providing drinking water. In many regions, however, the rate at which these aquifers are being exploited is higher than that at which they can naturally replenish their water supply.

What is aquifer recharging?

In order to counter the depleting stores of aquifer freshwater, authorities have been attempting to recharge aquifers using treated wastewater, injected or infiltrated directly into the aquifer system. Sounds like an inspired solution, yet concern has been raised over the safety of using reclaimed water, which if handled incorrectly, could potentially harm those who rely on aquifers for drinking water. Experts are concerned about the growing necessity of replenishing aquifer reserves, which are at risk from increasing salinisation if over-used, rendering them undrinkable.

Did you know? The overuse of aquifers in Indonesia's capital Jakarta has resulted in a level of salinisation which has crept 15 kilometres (10 miles) inland. Water in these areas is now undrinkable and huge investments have been required to build pipelines to carry water in from other areas.

Desalinisation

The desalinisation of seawater has become a viable solution to the growing demand for freshwater. Converting saltwater into freshwater for drinking or irrigation, desalinisation is a process now utilised worldwide, especially by the United Arab Emirates, Israel and the United States. Despite its increasing efficiency, however, the desalinisation process, known as reverse osmosis, still requires a significantly high input of electrical power, provided by non-renewable fossil fuels, which has caused concern as to the potential environmental and financial impact desalinisation may cause.

Price tag?

Desalinated water, due to its high level of energy consumption, is far more expensive than standard mains water. Although places such as Dubai and Saudi Arabia rely on desalinated water for 90% of their usage, desalinated water is only cost-effective in areas where there is no access to freshwater or where low-cost energy resources are available to fund the desalinisation process. It can be argued that the waste products from desalinisation can be recycled, but the overbearing costs of production make it a particularly expensive solution to the world's water crisis. Until desalinisation becomes

cost-effective, maximising energy efficiency, cheaper options such as the use of reclaimed water appear far more viable, especially with regards to agricultural and industrial demands.

Fact: There are over 13,000 desalinisation plants in the world.

The UK's first plant opened in Beckton, London in 2010. It can produce around 140 million litres a day by converting saltwater from the Thames to drinking water. The plant only takes in water on the outgoing tide, when it is a third as salty as normal seawater and so less energy is required to treat it.

The Jebel Ali Desalinisation Plant in the United Arab Emirates is the largest desalinisation plant in the world, and produces around 300 million cubic metres of water a year!

Resource pool

A list of useful organisations and companies*

*Please note: Information correct at time of printing

DEFRA

The Environment Agency

The Department for Environment, Food and Rural Affairs provides policy and legislation information on the natural environment, biodiversity, plants and animals, sustainable development and the green economy, food, farming and fisheries, animal health and welfare, environmental protection and pollution control.

DEFRA Customer Contact Centre
Noble House
17 Smith Square
London SW1P 3JR

Website: www.defra.gov.uk

Tel: 08459 33 55 77

The Environment Agency for England and Wales works to protect the environment and promote sustainable development. It works with partners to improve water quality across the UK, monitors flood risks and issues flood warnings.

The Environment Agency
National Customer Contact Centre
PO Box 544
Rotherham S60 1BY

Website:
www.environment-agency.gov.uk

Tel: 08708 506 506
Floodline: 0845 988 1188

The Scottish Environment Protection Agency

The Scottish Environment Protection Agency acts as an environmental regulator, helping business and industry to understand their environmental responsibilities and enabling customers to comply with legislation and good practice. It monitors flood risks in Scotland, and issues flood warnings.

SEPA Corporate Office
Erskine Court
Castle Business Park
Stirling
FK9 4TR

Website: www.sepa.org.uk

Tel: 01786 457700

Floodline: 0845 988 1188

The National Trust

This charity strives to conserve and protect woodland, fens, landscapes and beaches across England, Wales and Northern Ireland, including many of the rivers, ponds and lakes that supply us with fresh water.

The National Trust
PO Box 39
Warrington
WA5 7WD

Website: www.nationaltrust.org.uk

Tel: 0844 800 1895

The UK Groundwater Forum

The UK Groundwater Forum is an independent organisation that aims to raise awareness of groundwater and the role it plays in water supplies and the environment.

UK Groundwater Forum Secretariat
Maclean Building
Wallingford
Oxfordshire
OX10 8BB

Website: www.groundwateruk.org

World Water Assessment Programme

UNESCO's World Water Assessment Programme (WWAP) monitors freshwater issues globally in order to provide assessments and recommendations for governments at a national level.

WWAP Programme Office for
  Global Water Assessment
UNESCO
Villa La Colombella
Località di Colombella Alta
06134 Colombella
Perugia
Italy

Website: www.unesco.org/water/ wwap

Water UK

Water UK represents all UK water
and wastewater service suppliers
at national and European level,
providing a framework for the
water industry to engage with
government, regulators, stakeholder
organisations and the public.

Water UK
1 Queen Anne's Gate
London
SW1H 9BT

Website: www.water.org.uk

Tel: 020 7344 1844

WaterAid

This charity aims to improve
hygiene and water sanitation in
the world's poorest areas.

WaterAid
47-49 Durham Street
London
SE11 5JD

Website: www.wateraid.org

Tel: 020 7793 4594

Waterwise

The Water Footprint Network

This UK-based charity focuses on encouraging the UK to decrease its water consumption through education and raising awareness.

Waterwise
Camelford House
89 Albert Embankment
London
SE1 7TP

Website: www.waterwise.org.uk

Tel: 020 3463 2400

The Water Footprint Network (WFN) promotes the water footprint methodology (the amount of water used to produce the goods and services that a person/community consumes) as a way of establishing a sustainable, fair and efficient use of freshwater resources worldwide.

Water Footprint Network
c/o University of Twente
Horst Building
PO Box 217
7500 AE Enschede
The Netherlands

Website: www.waterfootprint.org

Tel: +31 53 489 4320

The Wildfowl & Wetlands Trust

Water and sewerage companies

The Wildfowl & Wetlands Trust (WWT) is a conservation organisation that aims to preserve wetlands and their wildlife.

**Wildfowl & Wetlands Trust
Slimbridge
Gloucestershire
GL2 7BT**

Website: www.wwt.org.uk

Tel: 01453 891900

Anglian Water:
www.anglianwater.co.uk

Dŵr Cymru/Welsh Water (DCWW):
www.dwrcymru.co.uk

Northern Ireland Water:
www.niwater.com

Northumbrian Water:
www.nwl.co.uk

Scottish Water:
www.scottishwater.co.uk

Severn Trent Water:
www.stwater.co.uk

Southern Water:
www.southernwater.co.uk

South West Water:
www.southwestwater.co.uk

Thames Water:
www.thameswater.co.uk

United Utilities:
www.unitedutilities.com

Wessex Water:
www.wessexwater.co.uk

Yorkshire Water:
www.yorkshirewater.com